Take Three Giant Steps!

A Vision 2030 Jamaica Reader

Collette D. Robinson

LMH PUBLISHING LIMITED

© 2014 Collette Robinson
First Edition
10 9 8 7 6 5 4 3 2 1

All rights reserved. No part of this book may be reproduced, stored in a retrieval system, or transmitted, in any form or by any means, electronic, mechanical, photocopying, recording, or otherwise, without the expressed written permission of the publisher or author.

All LMH Publishing Limited titles are available at special quantity discounts for bulk purchases for sales promotion, premiums, fund-raising, educational or institutional use.

This is a work of fiction. Names, characters, places and incidents either are the products of the author's imagination or are used fictitiously, and any resemblance to actual persons, living or dead, events or locales, is entirely coincidental.

Illustrations: Courtney Robinson
Editors: Dr. Adrian Mandara & K. Sean Harris
Cover Design: Sanya Dockery
Book Design, Layout & Typeset: Sanya Dockery

Published by: LMH Publishing Ltd.
Suite 10-11
Sagicor Industrial Park
7 Norman Road
Kingston C.S.O, Jamaica
Tel: 876-938-0005
Fax: 876-759-8752
Email: lmhbookpublishing@cwjamaica.com
Website: www.lmhpublishing.com

Printed in China   ISBN: 978-976-8245-21-2

NATIONAL LIBRARY OF JAMAICA CATALOGUING-IN-PUBLICATION DATA

Robinson, Collette D.
  Take three giant steps : a Vision 2030 Jamaica reader / Collette Robinson

  p. : col. ill. ; cm

ISBN 978-976-8245-21-2 (pbk)

1   Reader s (Secondary)   2.   Children's literature – Jamaica
I   Title

428.6   dc 23

Dedication

To my father, Joseph Ward, who instilled a love for the arts, music and culture in each of his children from an early age.

For Jamaica's children who with guidance and encouragement, can achieve their fullest potential and make Jamaica's Vision a reality.

Contents

Foreword

PART ONE

Chapter 1: Enter Manuel!   1

Chapter 2: A Purpose For a Boy   9

Chapter 3: The Place of Choice   15
    Song: Land My Love   22

Chapter 4: A Whole New Dream   25
    Dub Poetry: Boys!   32

Chapter 5: How Many Steps?   35
    Poem: If I can Dream   40

PART TWO

Chapter 6: A Boy and A Chance   45

Chapter 7: For All Jamaicans   53
    Song: We Strive!   58

Chapter 8: Values For Life   61

Chapter 9: Fit For a Country   69
    Poem: Protect Our Environment!   72

Chapter 10: Travel Economy Class!   75

Chapter 11: Three Giant Steps!   85
    Poem: The Sun's Day   93

Foreword

Although pitched for the Grade Six to Nine reader, this book is intended to reach the heart of anyone who takes it up. As a patriotic Jamaican who has shared in the framing of the Vision 2030 Jamaica, I felt the need to use my talents in an artistic and creative way to engage the imagination of our younger citizens. After all, the Jamaica we envisage in 2030 would largely be created by our efforts as working adults, yet would subsequently be enjoyed by our children and grandchildren. What we do now to create this ideal Jamaica is a legacy that we build and leave behind. Those who come after us will have to work equally hard to maintain the gains and to dream again.

Take Three Giant Steps! – a title based on a game I used to play long ago in my school playground back in

Mandeville – is first an educational work, introducing the major tenets of the long-term development plan for Jamaica in innovative ways. Secondly, it is a motivational work which will hopefully inspire our children to work and learn and make the most of all their opportunities. Finally, I would like to believe that this book will provide some fine examples of the use of words in literature, to make sights and sounds come alive, and reinforce some of the literature lessons.

The songs and poems have all been written by me and provide for engagement and interaction. I hope every child will find some value in these pages and every teacher will find some useful tools, as in my own way, I seek to share the message of the Vision 2030 Jamaica: "Jamaica, the place of choice to live, work, raise families and do business."

Collette D. Robinson

Part One

CHAPTER 1

Enter Manuel!

Manny flips the piece of broken glass expertly, flicking his wrist with his usual display of arrogance and poses, hands outstretched, as it settles neatly in the last box of the hopscotch game. "Ayeee!" he exclaims in a high-pitched screech, anticipating his pending victory. He begins to hop gleefully across the scorching hot pavement.

"Sound like a girl!" smirks Paula in disdain, knowing full well that her playmate is about to capture his second victory for the afternoon and none too pleased about it.

"Is you want me to play hopscotch with you though!" crows Manny happily as he picks up the piece of soda bottle and heads back to base triumphantly.

Game over, they both collapse wearily on the grass beside the concrete pavement, wishing the snow-cone man was around at that hour of the afternoon so they could cool their thirst. But the vendors at the school gate have long since packed up their leftover wares and taken their weary leave for another day. In fact, the schoolyard is strangely quiet with only a few children sitting around in the shade waiting for parents to pick them up, or for older siblings to exit their extra lessons.

Manny grimaces towards the fading sun. "Boy! It really hot! When your mother going to finish her meeting?" Paula smooths out her socks and brushes tiny wisps of dry grass from her shoes. "She soon come out. She talking to all the Grade Six teachers." Paula is stoutly proud of her mother who is the principal of their primary school. She glances at her unlikely playmate, a mischievous eleven year-old boy in tired khakis who had no qualms about beating the girls at their own games. "Where is your father?"

Manny relaxes on his elbows. "He around the back tidying up the P.E. room. He says I am to walk home with you and Miss Walters. He has to sweep up the school hall after that."

"And you need to go home and do your homework, right Manny?"

Manny laughs and hisses his teeth loudly. "I don't like to write composition and that is what Teacher want us to do for tomorrow. A story about how I spent the summer holidays." Manny shrugs. "I might do it or I might not. I will find some excuse."

"Manny, you don't realize that you are in Grade Six and you have to work harder than that?" Paula asks in as adult a tone as she can. "You not going to get into a good high school and get a good job when you grow big if you don't do your schoolwork now," she advises with all her Grade Five wisdom.

Manny snorts. "Is because your mother is a teacher why you saying that! Wait until you reach Grade Six, you will see is too much work! My father says I can do what I want and when I get big, I will find a job anyway."

"Why he don't help you with your homework?" asks Paula, spying her mother coming out of the staff room doorway. She gathers up her knapsack and lunch-bag as Manny scrambles to his feet as well.

"He can't read," he answers somberly, his mood changing swiftly, like the play of evening light and shadow across the playground. Manny, a chirpy, four-and-a-half feet bundle of energy has lived with his father all his life and still cannot get a straight answer when he asks where his mother is. He has heard that she moved away to another parish when he was very small. He feels sad about this sometimes and has vowed he will find her just as soon as he is big enough to leave home. He frowns a bit as the thought flashes through his mind. He has had to grow up very quickly and his nickname was given to him by some-one who felt he acted like a grown man sometimes, though it is also short for his given name, Manuel.

"Come on." Paula sets off in the direction of her mother, a tall, striking woman with a low-cut hairstyle who smiles in greeting as they all fall in step as they

leave the schoolyard and turn down the road towards home.

The road is quiet at this time of the afternoon, with most of the children having left for home from two o'clock. Quite a few of them live in Springland and the other communities nearby, but some have to go down the hill to the little square and take a bus to Spaldings or Christiana. Manny feels lucky to be able to simply walk home. He loves the peace and quiet of his little district and has not cared much for the rush and bustle of the town when he has had to go there with his father. A cool breeze is blowing now and the sun has gotten softer, a little smudged at the edges as Manny glances up at the sky.

Activity

a. Write down five things you already know about Manny.

b. Use a dictionary and search for the meaning of all the new words you have found.

CHAPTER 2

A Purpose For A Boy

The cool of the afternoon shade makes walking home a pleasant affair. Manny enjoys his companions and the feeling of being taken care of. He likes the attention that is drawn to them as the respected headmistress strides purposefully home. Everyone on the road has a word for her and horns toot as vehicles pass by.

"Come on Manuel, stay on the sidewalk...do I have to tell you that every day?" Miss Walters steers the boy to safety in front of her.

"No Miss, but nothing was coming."

"Mommy, Manny says he does not need to do his homework because he will grow up and get a job anyway," reports Paula, chuckling as she betrays her friend.

"Well, that all depends, I guess. What kind of job is Manny thinking about?" Miss Walters adjusts her handbag securely over her shoulder, and shifts the weight of the pile of books she is carrying to her other hip.

"Well, I want to maybe be a mechanic, or drive one of those fast taxis, or maybe I can be…a teacher like you!" Manny replies.

"And that is all good. But you need an education to do any of those. And the best education helps you to be the best at what you do," says the headmistress wisely. "And guess what? You can throw your net wider, just like the fishermen do down by the bay and be anything else you want to be. You could be a doctor, a musician, a businessman…whatever you can dream of. A good education will make it all possible."

Manny thinks on that for a while, matching his stride with Paula beside him. They hear excited voices from a familiar clearing out under some trees on the left and wave at Sheena and Tammy who are playing 'skip' with Annie to the little girl's delight. The swish of the rope punctuates their chants and laughter. "One, two, three Auntie Lulu!" fades slowly as the trio walk on.

"But Miss, my father don't have the money to keep me at school long you know. He tell me that everyday."

"Well Manuel, do your best now, learn all you can so you can do well in your examinations and get a place in high school. You are too young to worry about money. A whole lot of people have made good progress in life without starting out with a lot of money, boy. The first thing you need is ambition."

They walk in silence for a while, each lost in their own thoughts. Miss Walters helps them across the road carefully as they take the last turn toward the huddle of friendly-looking houses on Chalky Street where they call home.

Paula picks up on her train of thought as if there had been no break in the conversation. "Mommy, our

teacher says ambition gives poor people teeth! What does she really mean?" Manny listens intently as he pictures a huge set of teeth and restrains a giggle. He is also in a bit of doubt about this thing called ambition.

"Well, that is exactly what I was saying to Manuel. Some of us are not born into rich families, and have to struggle to find the basic things and send our children to school. But if we want better for ourselves and our children, and we work hard at it, and make sure our children use up all the opportunities they get for a good education, then it means we have ambition. We will work hard and succeed."

They reach Manny's gateway and prepare to separate. Miss Walters looks fondly at the young boy and thinks wistfully of the son she lost so many years ago. "Manuel, you go in and tidy up and have your supper. Then settle down and do your homework. We will meet you here in the morning, six-thirty as usual, okay? Tomorrow we have some people coming to school to tell us about the future of Jamaica, so that will be something exciting to look out for, okay?" She brushes his shoulder lightly in a quick goodbye and makes her way with Paula in tow to her own white picket gate a few steps away.

Manny steps briskly up the short walkway to his front door, retrieves the hidden key and lets himself in. He plans to eat and do his homework, but later. His father has left some rice and cornbeef on the small kerosene stove but Manny has other plans right now. He throws his worn schoolbag on the sofa, changes into yard clothes in a flash and heads for the back door. True to form, he hears chatter down by the big tree and runs quickly towards the sound of his friends, Marky and Slim, eager to resume their cricket match where they had left off the evening before. Manny's father would not be home for a good while, time enough to score a century off these two!

Activity

Unscramble the following words:

- DEIPR
- KDEOLWNEG
- YDIGNTI
- NISOVI
- OEPTNILAT
- LYAFMI
- MYOCEON
- ETCILMA
- NAPL
- SELAUV
- ECOHCI
- MTEIVRNONEN

CHAPTER 3

The Place of Choice

The schoolyard is a-buzz with excitement and columns and walkways are colourfully festooned with bright green, gold and black ribbons. A large map of Jamaica has been mounted on a chalkboard at the top of the stage where Devotions are set to begin in a moment. Below the map, some young enterprising artist has used coloured chalk to write "Jamaica, the place of choice to live, work, raise families and do business." Most of the older children read it aloud wondering what it means. Teachers are darting back and forth across the stage making last-minute changes to the preparations. Others are trying valiantly to keep the children – already stretched across the paved yard in long lines with their classmates – subdued and orderly. They are not having much success. The chatter is a steady drone, with

occasional peals of laughter. This morning the school has visitors from the Ministry of Education and they will be focusing on Jamaica's future.

There is a sudden hush as Miss Walters mounts the platform followed by some teachers and two other well-dressed persons. She uses the microphone and welcomes everyone with a proud beam on her face. Today, she says the school would be learning about Vision 2030 Jamaica. But first, they would have their usual devotions beginning with the National Anthem.

The children sing lustily to the brave accompaniment of the music teacher on the wheezy old piano perched in a corner of the platform. Paula glances accusingly at Manny in the next row as he hangs his head to hide his mumbling of the National Pledge that follows. She knows he still does not know the words properly. A bright little boy from Grade Four reads Psalm 100, and the Spanish Choir sings a song about "*Gracias a Dios*". Paula thinks it means "Thanks to God", and plans to ask her teacher later.

Finally, it is time to hear from the strangers on the platform and there is a stir of anticipation among the children, eager to hear what was new and get out of the morning sun. A short lady in a grey suit, introduced as Miss Blackwood, steps forward and begins to speak. She is from the Ministry of Education and is obviously a teacher too for she speaks in a simple and engaging way. All the children listen in rapt attention.

"In the same way that we have a National Anthem, a National Pledge, a National Motto and a National School Song, we now have a National Vision. This is a picture in our minds of what we want our country to be like. Right now, the Vision is for the year 2030, which may seem far away to you now, but will arrive quickly, one year at a time. By then you will be adults, working people, with your own children going to school.

"Our Vision says: 'Jamaica, the place of choice to live, work, raise families and do business'. We need to learn this by heart."

She has the children repeat it twice after her, and they settle again to listen.

"Our Vision means that every Jamaican, anywhere in the world, will be proud to say that our country is the best place in the whole world for people to live in, go to work, bring up their children and care for their elderly family members, and be successful if they choose to open a business. Everything that is necessary to make life easier would be in place, and people would feel safe and secure.

"It will take a lot of work for our country to reach that place by 2030. It will take a lot of hands working together, and many minds too. But we are a strong people, and our beautiful island has all it needs to make our vision come true. The most important thing about us is our people. From student to worker, from small farmer to big businessman, from towns to countryside, boys and girls, men and women of Jamaica will need to play our own small part in getting to where we want to be."

The flag-coloured ribbons rustle in the cool, early morning breeze and the early light brightens the upturned faces of the children. Some shuffle from one foot to another, but almost all are listening to the clear voice of the lady at the microphone. Manny thinks it all sounds very nice to think of Jamaica in that way, and to recognize that in 2030 he will be a big man. But he also wonders how he can do anything about helping his country if he and his father can hardly help themselves much. His mind wanders but a ripple of laughter from the group brings him back to the moment. He must have missed the joke for he sees his classmates smiling. Miss Blackwood is still speaking.

"By the time it reaches the year 2030, you will all be adults, many of you with your own children. Your parents will be elderly if they are still with us. This means that you will be the workers – policemen and women, nurses, business people, entertainers, farmers, teachers and more. You will be the main ones earning money to meet your families' needs, and to do everything else.

"But you cannot reach very far without a good education. Even after leaving high school, you have to

get enough training in the skill or profession you like so that you can make good products or give good quality service. Even though you are young people, it does not mean that you are to stop learning. You must grab every chance you get to learn more about the world and about your own skill. You will be able to do this through studying at different schools, attending training, and even using the Internet and reading a lot.

"The new Vision that we have for our schools and other places that offer teaching, is to make sure that every child does well. Our government will ensure that our schools have the equipment they need and that teachers have all the materials they need."

There is a low grumble and rustle from the group of teachers at the back, and Miss Blackwood gives an understanding smile. "The government will also continue to help those who are from poor families to have what they need for school. In our schools we have to keep the place clean and healthy, as well as safe for all children. Some children have disabilities which mean they may need special help to use the school. We have to help all those children to feel happy and to be able to learn and play with us. They will also need to get more education and good jobs too when they grow up." Manny glances at Chad in the row ahead of him leaning on his crutch with one-legged arrogance and smiling. Chad is such a part of everything. He is faster than us and we don't even remember sometimes that he has only one leg, he thinks soberly. He is really fun. Miss Blackwood is still speaking.

"We want all our schools and colleges to be the best in the Caribbean and the world. And when we graduate from them we want to be the best example of what students and workers should be like," she announces.

After a few more words the headmistress thanks the guests and explains that they will go around and visit the Grades Five and Six classrooms and speak a bit more to the older children during the morning. The children are dismissed to return to their classrooms and they file past the group of teachers slowly, before breaking into a noisy run for their classrooms.

Song: Land My Love!

(to the tune of Yellow Bird)

Land my love!
I see you in Vision bright!
Bold and free!

Ablaze with a vibrant light!
People warm of heart, though they are miles apart
Come together now, share the dream somehow!
This is our land, we will take a stand!
Make our Vision come true!

Land my love!
There's so much you have to give!
Blend our hearts!
And give us the will to live!
Though we're young at heart, we can make a start!
Lift our head up high! Strength to signify!
Build Jamaica up!
Father, fill our cup!
Make our Vision come true!

Collette Robinson
December 2010

Activity

Sing the song!

CHAPTER 4

A Whole New Dream

The children hush into silence half an hour later as the lady from the Ministry makes her stop at the Grade Six classroom. The stern look on their teacher's face belies the twinkle in her eyes. She too is pleased at the company and the excitement the visit has created in the school that morning. "Now, now students," she croons, "let's settle down in our seats and listen to what Miss Blackwood has to say. I am sure we have already learned something new today. And that's a good way to start the day, don't you think?" Miss Turner always speaks in perfect English, and many of the children try hard to be like her. She beams a welcome to the visitor and offers her a seat next to her at the shiny wooden table stacked with books and chalk boxes.

"Since you all are the oldest ones in the school, and

will soon be taking exams and moving on to new schools, it is important that you understand a bit more about the vision for Jamaica, and how you will become a part of it," Miss Blackwood begins. She repeats the slogan that is so beautifully written on the chalkboard outside, and allows the class to repeat after her. She speaks for a little about why all Jamaicans should want to live in a better society, and how it would mean better lives for everyone. She reminds the class that in the blink of an eye, they would be the adults who would be working and sending their own children to school. Manny closes his eyes for an instant trying to imagine himself as an adult. The good thing is I wouldn't have to be in school, he smiles to himself, lost in his daydream.

Miss Blackwood is still speaking and Manny jerks his attention back to her.

"When someone is not able to afford to meet their own needs for food and shelter everyday, it means they are living in poverty. Of course, food and shelter are just the first set of needs that have to be met for people to live. Other important needs are health care, education, and just being able to know and understand what is taking place around us. We call that need 'information' and it is very important.

"At this time in Jamaica, about fourteen out of every hundred persons are living in poverty. Persons who study poverty all across the world tell us that in a family, poverty can be like a wheel. That means you are never quite sure where it begins or ends. This is because the things that cause poverty also look like the results of being in poverty. It is like looking through both sides of a clear piece of glass – you see the same picture. Here are some examples: not enough education; no skills to get a good job; low wages and not enough jobs around. These things may cause poverty, but they also describe what happens when people are in poverty.

"How do we get outside of this wheel of poverty if we belong to such a family? Getting a good education is the first and best answer. Learning and doing well at school will open the door for better chances in life. These chances will include higher education, finding good jobs that pay well, and being able to meet all those basic needs we looked at and lots more!"

After this mouthful Miss Blackwood and Miss Turner take questions from the class which is still lively and talkative. Mostly the girls are the ones who

ask questions. Manny feels a bit timid and decides he will ask the principal to explain some things to him later.

The other lady from the Ministry has finished with the Grade Five classes and joins the group in the classroom. She is a younger woman with a lively-looking face and dancing eyes. She tells the class they are going to learn a poem and she hands out pieces of paper with type-written lines. The children read it quickly, and Miss Jones, that is her name, explains

that it is 'dub poetry' which will require the boys to do a bit of drumming on their desk tops to keep the rhythm going. Manny perks up at this. He enjoys drumming, but the teacher has never allowed them to use their desks for this purpose. This is indeed a special morning!

Miss Jones takes a few moments to talk about the poem, which is called 'Boys!'. She talks about the great potential of boys and how important they are in the society. She laments the number of boys who

get themselves in trouble by being involved in misconduct of all kinds: in their homes, schools and communities. Miss Jones believes that when boys realize what they can achieve, and bend their minds to getting a good education, the society will be better off in many ways, including the showing of respect to girls and women. She encourages all the boys in the class to spend time on their lessons, especially because they were nearing examination time, and noted that she expected to hear great things about them in the future.

Miss Jones then reads the poem aloud, bouncing between the aisles of the classroom as the children catch on to the rhythm. The girls clap to the beat while Manny and some of the other boys bang out a rhythm on the top of their desks. Miss Turner smiles and joins in the fun, and at the end, she declares they will work on it some more and maybe enter it in the school festival later in the year. The class is delighted, thoroughly enjoying the change in routine this morning.

Dub Poetry: Boys!

Boys, boys!
Big up the boys!
Raise up your hand and make some noise!
'Man pon the land!'
Taking a stand!
Strength and vision and positive vibes!

Boys, boys!
Big up the boys!
Full respect and the girls are not toys!
Blend and commend!
Stand by your friend!
Growing together with honour and poise!

Boys, boys!
Big up the boys!
Raise up your hand and make some noise!
Ready, Set, Go!
Success to show!
Jamaica's future, shining with pride!

Collette Robinson
December 2010

Activity

Recite the poem with drum beat accompanying the voices. Use creative ways to mimic a drum beat.

CHAPTER 5

How Many Steps?

The courtyard is noisy at lunchtime as both children and teachers mill about. Some are getting their lunches at the canteen window to the left of the hall, while others sit under the shade of the large blue mahoe tree, chattering and eating from lunch-bags. The teachers huddle together at the classroom doors, exchanging news and laughing loudly. Miss Walters waves goodbye to the Ministry van as it crawls through the school-gate, carefully avoiding the groups of children at play. Manny washes down his school lunch with the last swig from his box juice, and wipes his mouth furtively on his sleeve. "Manny, I saw that!" yells Paula, as she runs past to join her friends at the far end of the yard. Both boys and girls have clustered around watching the progress of 'how many steps to reach the King'. Tony is the 'king' this time and he is making a meal of it. Manny and Paula run to the sidelines to watch.

Lunchtime is almost over and the game has become frenzied as three children vie for the honour of reaching the king first. Tony is having the time of his life, chortling with laughter as he picks and chooses who to favour. "Take two baby steps!" he giggles at Sasha, who grimaces with disgust since she sees clearly that this will not help her to reach much further. "Take three giant steps!" he dares Mikey, who stretches so hard with his short, plump legs that he rips his pants to the extreme delight of everyone. Manny laughs loudly. I could have done that he thinks, if it were me. I could have won with three giant steps. Tony's best friend Leroy wins the game easily with six frog leaps and the group scatters to get ready for the last session of the school-day.

As he walks home with Miss Walters and Paula later that afternoon, Manny tells the teacher he had a good day. "So did I Manuel but a rather tiring one too," she replies. "And what did you think of our visitors? Did you learn something new today?"

"Lots of things Miss," replies Manny, glancing at Paula with a warning in his eyes. He did not want his little friend to betray him. She smiles, hopping along

to keep up with her mother. "I learned the Vision by heart," she announces proudly. Manny gives her a 'monkey face' when her mother is not looking and vows to learn it by heart himself as soon as he can. "How about you Manuel?" Miss Walters prompts.

"Well, I think it was interesting. The school was pretty and I liked the music. And I like some of the things that the lady tell us," he begins.

"Told us," corrects Miss Walters, "go on".

"Yes, well, I would like Jamaica to be like what she says. And I would like to be able to grow big and start to work and earn money so I can have nice things, and help my father. She said we can be anything we want to be as long as we stay in school and learn. I can be a fireman, or a police, or a teacher like you Miss, or even a pilot!"

Miss Walters chuckles. "Yes Manuel, you can be anything you want, go anywhere on the wings of education. Don't limit yourself to what you see around you now. There is a lot more to see out in the world as you grow older and wiser, and learn more. You can succeed at something good as long as you put your mind to it. It does not matter if you are from a poor or humble home. What is important is what you

do with the brain God gave you. Think big! When everybody plays their part – Government, community, church, family – you will have the opportunity to do well. But it will take hard work."

She pauses to cross the children safely to the other side of the road and they continue homeward. She waves at a friendly toot in her direction by a passing taxicab laden with chattering passengers. The trio saunter alongside the grassy embankment and Paula bends to brush her hand along a sprig of 'shame ol' lady', giggling with delight as the tiny leaves close and huddle together in response. "How come they do that Mommy?" she asks. Her mother tells her it is nature's design.

Manny thinks about what Miss Walters has said, and feels hopeful. He really believes his principal. If she was that positive about what he could achieve in spite of not having a lot of money, then he was going to give it a try. After all, he was not one for allowing anyone to beat him, unless he wanted to. He felt a bright, warm feeling as he thought about what he had learned that day. It has been an enjoyable day, he muses as he skips to keep up with his company. Take three giant steps indeed, he challenges himself.

"I can do that!"

Poem: If I Can Dream

If I can hold a dream within my palm
And spin it 'round, or toss it to and fro…
But keep it safe and hidden in my heart
And nurture it, and watch it sprout and grow…

If I allow my dream to touch my heart,

And know that my own vision can be real…
That with my soul, and all the gifts I have
I can become whatever I may feel…

Then… I can rise above my circumstance
And bear my dream aloft to dizzy heights!
I'd strive for excellence with every chance!
And make my dream come true, in brilliant lights!

Collette Robinson
January 2011

Activity

a. How do you feel about this poem?

b. Do you have a dream of what you would like to be? Write one paragraph about it.

c. Recite the poem!

Part Two

CHAPTER 6

A Boy and A Chance

Miss Dean snips the dried leaves from her treasured rose patch and wonders whether it is time to spray for pests again. Nothing must happen to these roses, she vows, as she ponders what she will enter in the garden show this year. Snippety-snip! She winces at a thorn prick and steps back to view her handiwork. The early light and mist of the spring morning are the perfect backdrop for her rose garden and she smiles in satisfaction. She tucks a wisp of grey hair further under her scarf, and looks around for the watering can a few feet away on the driveway. It is cool this morning. She hears the creak of the front door and quick footsteps down the steps and turns as the child moves quickly towards her.

"Had your breakfast Manny?" she asks, knowing

full well he would never leave for school without it.

"Sure, Aunt Dean, and I'm leaving now."

" Stay out of the sun today, because you know you have a cold." He gives his grand-aunt a hug and slips through the squeaky little iron gate to the side of the garden, on to the street nearby. "Good morning Mister Charlie," he calls to the neighbour on the other side, also out strolling in his garden. He receives a cheerful answer. Mr. Charles watches Manny stride down the street, opens his gate and comes to have a chat with Miss Dean, his neighbour of many years.

"What a mannersable little chap, eh?" he says in his quavering tone, admiring the lovely roses Miss Dean is tending. "Certainly a promising fellow." The elderly gentleman balances himself on his knobbly walking stick.

"Yes, he's doing pretty well at school too. See how much he's grown in the past year! And he is good company," she answers.

"So does he take the bus down when he reaches the main road?" Mr. Charles asks. Miss Dean explains that most times Manny simply walks to school because he loves the early morning breeze and the freedom of moving at his own pace. "I think it reminds him of the countryside and I know he misses that." She

gathers her garden tools together as she speaks. The neighbours chat for a while more then separate as Miss Dean prepares to go inside for her morning coffee.

Hope Meadows is a huge, sprawling community a mile from Liguanea in St. Andrew, built some time in the 1970s. The houses look similar to each other, set back from the roadway behind large lawns and a variety of gardens. Some houses are freshly painted, while others look a little tired, patchy in places with scarred paint and drooping iron gates. The street is quiet at this time of the morning with the occasional car swishing by in search of a short-cut to the main street ahead. Manny walks briskly, his knapsack over his right shoulder and his arms deep in his pockets. He has grown over the past year, stretching above most of his classmates in Grade Seven, with a lanky look, and an easy-going style.

As he walks down the main street towards Mona

College, his new high school, he wonders what his father is doing at that moment. He misses him, but is really enjoying high school in Kingston and living with his grand-aunt has been a good experience so far. He remembers with a smile the day that the examination results had come out and he found out he was going to be attending May Pen High. Then his father's aunt had contacted him saying she would love if Manuel could come to Town and live with her for a while. She would make sure he went to school there, while providing him with everything he needed. Manny's father had jumped at the chance for the little boy to have a better life than he could afford. Miss Walters, the principal at his primary school, had been quick to assist the family to get Manny transferred to Mona College, a well known boy's high school. That was almost a year ago and now Manny was coming to the end of Grade Seven.

Manny thinks fondly of Springland and looks forward to his next week-end visit at mid-term. He enjoys living in Hope Meadows, perhaps because it has so many trees and flowers and is still not too near to the bustling city. Living with his aunt has been good, and his father says that he has grown about six inches since he turned twelve. His father says it must be the food and care that he is getting from his aunt, plus the fact that he is turning into a teenager.

Manny turns to cross at the school crossing, waiting with a group of chattering boys who have just alighted from the puffing bus heading up to Papine. The school crosser steps out smartly in his bright yellow vest, holding up his sign, and the boys move across in a noisy, excited herd. Manny heads quickly towards the First Form Block. Today is Jamaica Day and it is going to be an exciting one.

Activity

a. Look at the first paragraph. Write down four things you learn about Miss Dean right away.
b. Write down all the words in the chapter that tell you about a sound.

CHAPTER 7

For All Jamaicans

It is mid-morning and the school has settled into its usual rhythm. But something is different today and the energy can be heard and felt. Each of the Grades has been asked to conduct an activity based on celebrating Jamaica Day in a form of their own choosing but with the National Motto as the theme: 'Out of many, one People'. Some classes are having debates, some have a concert going on, some have a quiz competition, and others are using various kinds of drama and music to depict the theme.

The noise level in the school is a little higher than usual but the principal, Mr. Bell, strolls around listening and observing, ignoring the noise with a satisfied look on his face. He is a tall, reed-thin man, with dark-rimmed glasses hanging from a cord around his neck, which he rarely uses. The students feel he wears them only when he wants to look very strict. Right now he is just enjoying the activities each class is engaged in.

Manny's class has decided to show the different races that live in Jamaica. They have learned about this in History class and have broken up into groups to plan for the event. Their own class theme is 'Out of Many, we are one! Every race and colour under the sun!' Their History teacher has helped them to identify several races of people living in Jamaica. She calls it ethnic background. Each group has done some research, created a poster, and helped with a small exhibition in a corner of the classroom. Manny is in the Chinese group, but there is also the Indian, African, Lebanese and Caucasian. The class has settled on these as the major ones. At Nikkosi's insistence – they call him Jah Teen – the class has included Rastafari. Manny's classroom is a blaze of colour. The boys have pulled out all the stops and shown their artistic talent, with the help of some teachers, of course.

The presentations begin and the boys enjoy it all. Some of the presenters use drama to tell about how their group arrived in Jamaica and try to speak with appropriate accents that they feel represent them. The class roars with laughter as Manny, straight-faced, reels

off the history of the Chinese in Jamaica with a strong Mandarin accent. After all the groups present, Miss Bryan, the form teacher, gets them to calm down and take their seats so she can wrap up the session. She wants to make some important points, she says, so that the entire class can learn from the experience, as much as they had enjoyed it.

"Remember our vision for Jamaica? The place of

choice to live, work, raise families, and do business? That vision is for all of us, every Jamaican family. It does not matter what our colour is, whether we are of Indian, or Chinese descent, or otherwise. We all should have the same rights and opportunities here and we all should feel comfortable living together, knowing that the country belongs to all of us. Anyone of us can do well at what we put our minds to and we all should be interested in how our country makes progress." She looks at Richard, nicknamed Jackie Chan. Manny thinks all the boys in school have a nickname, at least the popular boys. His own is Countryman, and he doesn't mind at all. Miss Bryan observes, "For example, we know many Jamaicans of Chinese descent own stores and shops and other business places. But we have to make sure, as a country, that they are also accepted in other ways, and can enjoy all the aspects of life in Jamaica. So too the Lebanese, or the Indians. The cultures and traditions may be different, but no one race is more Jamaican than the other. We all belong."

Miss Bryan glances at Nikkosi, patiently waiting for her to weave him in, and smiles. "Rastafari is a very important part of our culture, even though it is not a race. It is like a part of the African heritage but very distinct. What is most important in this 'one Jamaica'

are some basic values that we all should share. Respect for each other, hard work, honesty, truth, national pride, cooperation, trust and responsibility." She pronounces each value slowly, as if to make it sink in. "Those are some of the values on which we can build our society and live in peace together, even with our differences. Whatever you learn from adults please do not learn prejudice. You are the youth and the future. You have the chance to truly unite all Jamaicans."

After a few more points, the teacher allows the

boys to go for lunch, after which they will have the chance to look around at the exhibits in other classrooms. Manny hails his friend Lenny as they head for the school canteen. Boys are milling around heading in all sorts of directions across the schoolyard. Manny still misses not having girls at school but he is getting used to it. He remembers Aunt Dean telling him she thought boys learned better on their own. She had been a teacher, she should know.

Song: We Strive!
(to the tune of the National School Song)

1
We wake up to the sunrise
That greets a brand new day!
So filled with hope and promise!
Our Deity sends our way!
    We join our hands together
    And work, and play and serve!
    Fulfilling all our passion,
    One nation, our resolve!
And so, with pride and energy
Our tasks we must complete

And building on our history
Our goals we strive to meet!

2

And with the glimpse of sunset
When weary toil is o'er
We pause to count our blessings
And new strength to implore.

    Our will, our gifts, our talents
    The courage that we feel,
    Will harness our resilience,
    Our shoulder to the wheel!

And so, in love and unity
Our Vision to create
We strive with power and dignity
And make our nation great!

Collette Robinson
January 2011

Activity

a. What do you think of the words of the song?
b. Sing the song!

CHAPTER 8

Values For Life

"Countryman, you coming to basketball practice later?" Manny nods to his friend Sherman as he bounces by his table in the packed canteen. Manny enjoys the freedom of lunchtime, and digs hungrily into his meal of fried chicken, vegetables and rolls. Basketball is his favourite sport, although the boys tease him that he is too short for that game. Coach says he is doing really well though and he smiles as he recalls his former principal, Miss Walters, encouraging him not to limit himself. "Always try something new," she had said, " something that will challenge you." It had been a good year in Grade Seven so far.

At the table Manny's friends are finishing up their lunch, laughing and chatting in between bites. They are as different as their faces. Malcolm, who lives in the Maxfield area, is tall and lanky, already with a gruff voice that sometimes ends in a squeak. Lenny is from somewhere near to Papine and walks to school as well. He is soft-spoken and loves to read. Jackie Chan, who is already thirteen years old, wears glasses and gets A's in everything. Ruel is from Russell Heights, and his father drops him at school every morning. He always has enough lunch money, something Manny still finds strange. Since coming to live in Town, Manny has learned about the inner city, and uptown and downtown, ideas that were different from his life back home. Here at school it is no problem though. The boys feel quite okay being friends with each other and they enjoy each other's company and the tales they have to share. They have good times together, these four.

    Later, after school, Manny changes quickly into his shorts and T-shirt and heads for the basketball court, which is actually inside the huge school hall. The roof of the hall is very high, and it gives an airy feeling to the place. Some boys at the far end are playing ping-pong, while a bunch of others struggle to bring the huge bundles of cricket gear out of the storage area and through the doors to the field outside. P.E.

teachers are everywhere, shouting orders above the din and getting ready for the afternoon's many sporting activities. Manny loves this about his school. Mona College is known to excel in several sports and lots of trophies and medals line the walls above the raised platform. Manny hopes one day to have his name carved on one of the huge, polished notice-boards, champion something or the other.

The basketball coach arrives some ten minutes later and the team assembles to the side of the court for their usual talk. Mr. Allen, the coach, a young man who looks about seven feet tall, at least to Manny, always gives the boys a pep talk before the exercises and the training session begin. "Boys, as I said last time, sports allow you the chance to learn a lot about life. In order for you to do well, you have to be part of the team. Although you are on a team, each person still has a role to play. If the centre does not provide enough cover, then the wing and guard players cannot do their jobs. At the same time, you have to be disciplined. You have to follow the plan, or the tactic of the game. You also have to move on quickly, even after a mistake has been made. You have no time while you are in the game to dwell on your mistakes. And very importantly, some team is going to lose. Take your loss with a good spirit, having done your best in the game. Then you take some time, as we will after this session, to look at what you may have done wrong, or where you may have made a poor choice or decision. Those are lessons for life. Okay fellows? Let's get some stretches done."

The boys scatter to do their exercise routine. Manny thinks Mr. Allen has said some very wise words. He is still thinking about this a couple of hours later as he and Lenny make their weary way up the hill towards home. The sunset makes the evening sky look streaky and beautiful with bright gold and pink staining the fluffy clouds. Just like back home in the countryside, Manny enjoys the natural beauty, and has even taught his city-born friend Lenny to share in the delight. The evening hours are much cooler. The boys talk about their day as the busy street fills with vehicles whizzing by in both directions. They wave at Buckley on the corner, trying to sell the last of his cane and fruit from the back of his battered old van before calling it a day. He has been on that corner for years Lenny tells Manny, faithfully selling fresh fruit to all who care to buy.

"Tomorrow is that Science test," Lenny reminds

his friend, as they prepare to split up at the Hope Meadows intersection. "Remember to revise what we learned about the environment."

"Sure," Manny replies, "after I get a good dinner into my stomach." The boys part ways and Manny turns onto the Boulevard, walking more rapidly as he nears home. Miss Dean is in the kitchen when he enters and greets him with a smile. "How was school, boy? Come and tell me all about this Jamaica Day thing that had you so excited. Wash up your hands and I will get your dinner on the table." Manny is quick to obey, catching sight of some large dumplings swimming with some slices of yam in the big pot, and smelling the unmistakeable aroma of pot stew. His stomach churns hungrily as he lands his knapsack on the floor of his room and dashes to wash his face and hands. He is going to have a lot to tell his grand-aunt and he plans to colour it with drama. He also plans to give her a blow by blow description of the basketball game which his team had won, with the help of six points from himself. Afterwards, he knows he will help to tidy the kitchen, watch the television news and then settle to his bath, homework and sleep.

Activity

a. What are values?
b. Which values has this chapter identified? Draw a picture or a diagram that shows them.

CHAPTER 9

Fit for a Country

Later that night Miss Dean settles down to a quiet read of the newspaper after Manny has gone to bed. She too loves the relaxing atmosphere of Hope Meadows, near enough to the busy city, but cradled by lush trees and bushes, giving a feel of the countryside. While the days were sunny, the nights are cool. She tucks her old woolen shawl across her knees and hoists her legs up unto the hassock as she thumbs through the pages of the daily papers. Although she cannot move around as much as she used to, she makes sure to get her newspapers from the boy at the corner every morning. Miss Dean had been a teacher of Geography, and she still loves to read. She hisses her teeth in disgust at some of the headlines, snorts loudly at a few and decides to read through the Disaster Awareness magazine tucked inside the last section.

Outside, the crickets are beginning a lively chorus of loud chirps as darkness envelopes the skies.

Most of the articles are on climate change and how what was happening globally would affect Jamaica and other small islands. There is an article about how global warming was causing sea levels to rise and what this could result in. Another article looks at temperature rise and the effect on weather patterns. There are pictures of disasters caused by hurricanes and flooding in various parts of Jamaica. Another interesting article about developments on the island's coasts and some of the risks that this created for the coral reefs and the mangroves catches her eye. Miss Dean becomes so engrossed in her reading she is unaware of how late it has become. The soft chimes of the old clock remind her it is eleven o' clock. She catches sight of an article titled *Vision 2030 and Climate Change* and decides to see what the country intends to do about managing climate change.

The article describes how climate change is caused mainly through increased carbon dioxide in the atmosphere, leading to a warming of the earth's temperature. This gives rise to increased weather activity such as hurricanes, droughts, even earthquakes.

Small islands in the Caribbean are most prone to disasters caused by the changes in weather and therefore, she reads, it is going to be very important that plans are in place to reduce the risk of these disasters. The article goes on to describe some strategies that Jamaica will have to put in place to manage the process of climate change and to reduce any hazards that arise from it. These include making sure all the citizens have good, accurate information. There will also be greater attention paid to where people build their houses, so that there is less risk of flooding and loss of life. Some persons are going to need to be re-located to safer areas. The government will have to carefully consider the physical location of highways and hotels and other investments, so that the natural resources of the country can be preserved. The article also mentions improving responses to emergencies, and taking part in world-wide efforts to reduce carbon dioxide in the atmosphere.

    Miss Dean stretches. Just one or two more paragraphs and she will call it a day, she decides. The same article goes on to describe how Jamaica will be by 2030. Miss Dean smiles to herself. She figures she may not be around then but she certainly wants Manny to enjoy life in a better Jamaica than she has yet seen. She reads the last of the article.

"Our society needs to put in place the types of laws, regulations, policies and programmes that protect or reduce exposure to these risks. Hand in hand with the care and preservation of the natural environment, efforts at preventing and reducing hazard risks will require high levels of awareness and deliberate action. Some of what we need to do may be difficult at first but will benefit our people in the end."

Miss Dean nods in agreement with this and plans to have Manny read it for himself the next day. She puts the magazine aside on the centre table so it will not get tossed out with the rest of the newspaper. Weary now, she struggles out of the warm sofa, and totters down the hallway to her bedroom.

Poem: Protect Our Environment!

Room for rent – apply within!
People deserve a place fit to live in!
Riverbed Way and Gullybank Lane!
Careful we don't wash away in the rain!

Room for rent – apply within!
Children healthy and the place well clean!
All of the garbage sorted and stowed
Some on the compost, none on the road!

Room for rent – apply within!
Climate change is a serious thing!
More hurricanes can lead to disaster!
We have to plan now, or we will suffer after!

Room for rent – apply within!
Coasts and reefs and urban planning!
Up on the hill, down in the catchment
Preserve and protect our environment!

Collette Robinson
December 2009

Activity

a. How do you feel about this poem?
b. Discuss each verse.
c. Write out all the words that relate to the environment, and look for their meaning in your dictionary.

CHAPTER 10

Travel Economy Class!

It is a week later and Manny is excitedly putting his things together to head out for school. This morning the class will be taking a field trip with their Geography and Social Studies teachers, and it promises to be a great break from the routine school day. The class has been learning about primary, secondary and tertiary industries, and today they will get to actually see some examples of these. He bids a cheerful goodbye to his aunt, busy in her garden as usual. This morning the birds perched atop the telephone lines strung between the lightposts are chattering even louder than normal as a gentle breeze stirs the trees. Manny has an extra spring in his step today as he heads down the street towards his school.

After roll-call and devotions the boys gather in front of the school hall to pile into the brightly coloured yellow bus that is parked and waiting. They want to get an early start for today they are going out of town to visit a farm, a processing factory, a cannery and a large retail supermarket. They are going to follow the chain of industries, and see how it works. Miss Rowe, the Geography teacher, says that after today they will have a better appreciation of how food gets to their plate. More importantly, they will understand how industries are linked together. She expects the day to be a great learning experience for them all and expects them to take notes of important points that they would want to remember. Manny takes a seat up front, near to the driver. He likes to watch as the driver changes the gears, muscles rippling in his huge arm, as he skillfully steers the wheel with his other hand. The young boy is still intrigued with driving.

It does indeed turn out to be a wonderful day. The class first visits a large vegetable farm in St. Ann where carrots, lettuce, callaloo, potatoes, onions and other small crops are grown. They are given a tour of some of the fields, and some of the boys even enjoy a tractor ride. They are shown the greenhouses that protect the young plants and the way the fields are kept irrigated. They help the farmer to shell some gungo peas and he is delighted with their assistance. They are also shown some small livestock such as chickens and goats on a neighbouring farm. Before they leave for their next stop the farmer treats them to cups of delicious soup. Manny and his friends enjoy the soup, creamy and full of vegetables and chicken. Manny remembers how he used to ask his father what was

in the soup that was their meal so often and how his father would say, "Drink up yuh soup boy! Is mix up soup!"

Their next stop is a cannery in St. Catherine. The factory workers are cooking and preparing vegetables for canning. The foreman, who is expecting the group, takes them through the process from beginning to end. They see where the vegetables are delivered to the factory from several farms, how they are sorted, cleaned and packaged for cooking. They meet different workers who take charge of the various stages of processing, all of them in aprons and with their heads covered. The boys are also shown all the equipment that is used at each stage. At the very end, they see the cans of vegetables rolling out to be packed into boxes. It is very exciting. There are cans with carrots, cans with peas, and cans with mixed vegetables. The experience leaves the boys very hungry and they are delighted to learn that the factory canteen has prepared lunch for them. It turns out to be a delicious and nutritious meal of baked chicken, vegetables and mashed potatoes which Manny and his friends enjoy whole-heartedly.

To complete the learning exercise, the students then visit a large supermarket on the Boulevard as they make their way back into Kingston in the early afternoon. Here they are again introduced to the entire process of delivery of goods, checking and packing, and then the display of the items on the shelves. Neat rows of canned vegetables and meats are stacked high along the shelves. Next door, in a fairly large restaurant known as the Deli, the boys see

the final leg of the process where the meat and vegetables are being made into sumptuous meals and sandwiches, including patties, for which a line of customers is patiently waiting. The boys are allowed to purchase what they want from the supermarket or the Deli and Manny buys a vegetable patty, piping hot and delicious. As they re-group outside, Miss Rowe reminds them that they have now seen examples of

primary, secondary and tertiary industries in agriculture. The students can think of many other examples just by looking at the supermarket shelves.

In the bus, the teacher talks a bit about how the different parts of the economy work together for the good of the country.

"When we talk about our 'economy' we are looking at all the ways that goods (such as food, clothes, machines and so on), and services (such as banking, education, hospital care, tourism and so on) are produced. All these examples make up the economy. We can think of many more examples. What is important is that when goods and services are produced, they are sold for money and that is how our country earns an income. Everyone who sells goods or services and makes money adds to the wealth of the country. It is this income that goes back into providing some of the things that we all need, such as roads, water, bridges and hospitals.

"In order for our economy to be strong we need to make sure that several things are in place. Some of these are: good transportation, use of modern equipment, easy ways to borrow money for business, and enough electricity and water. You have seen the different industries at work today in just one example – how food is produced. We saw agriculture, agri-processing, manufacturing, wholesale and retail distribution. Because we are a small island, we need to buy goods and services from abroad sometimes. We also want business people from abroad to come and open businesses, for example factories and hotels in our country. When they do this, it means more jobs for our people. You have seen the linkages today, one industry needs others, and more people are able to find jobs. We also need to make it easy and interesting for business people to want to produce goods and services here. That is called investment. All of these things are important for our economy to be strong. A strong economy is the first thing we need for Jamaica to be a developed country by 2030."

After that, Miss Rowe settles down to enjoy the rest of the drive back to school. The boys chatter around her and the bus puffs its way through the traffic that is building on the city streets. It has really been a good day and she is sure the boys have learned something through the experience of actually seeing what they had only been reading of before in their textbooks.

Activity

a. What are some of the sectors in the economy?
b. Think of two other examples of primary, secondary and tertiary industries that link to each other.
c. Work in groups and do a skit about working in a selected sector of the economy.

CHAPTER 11

Three Giant Steps!

It will soon be time to go home for the holidays and although Manny loves his school, his heart bursts with the anticipation of a few weeks to spend in the countryside. He has so much to share with Paula and his other friends, and they are always so happy to see him, his father too, though he tries to hide his happiness by being gruff with the boy. Manny understands his father much better now and he knows he will be bringing home a good Report. The last of the school tests are complete and he thinks he did well in all his subjects. He has a different view of school than he had when he was younger ever since he had challenged himself that he would take those three giant steps and be a successful student.

Today is the day for the huge Peace and Love concert in the school hall and the most exciting part is that other high schools nearby have been invited to send some of their students. That means girls would be around and some of the boys think that is pretty exciting. A couple of well known entertainment artistes, like D'Range and DJ Plus, will be there, as well as school talent. Manny feels a nervous rumble in his stomach, and hopes he will do his entertainment piece well. He has been practising it for some time now with the help of his Drama teacher. The students stream into the hall finding their favourite seats and chattering noisily above the sound of reggae music coming through the huge speakers to the sides of the hall. A slim-built young man is testing microphones on the stage while another fellow is securing lengths of wire across the floor. It is a beehive of activity. Some boys are hanging the brightly-coloured school banner on top of the stage while two struggle with a life-sized Perky Parrot, the Peace mascot.

The older boys at Mona College are responsible for putting the event together. In Devotions some weeks before, they had told the rest of the school that they were concerned about how children deal with problems, and that there were too many incidents where children were hurting each other in schools. They wanted to encourage children to live in peace together and to solve any conflicts by talking about it with someone who could help. The boys, mostly in Sixth Form, had spoken about the kinds of values and attitudes that children needed to have if Jamaica was to become a developed country. Mr. Bell felt very proud of them as they spoke and the rest of the school had been excited to hear about the coming concert.

It is finally here Manny thinks, looking around at the tide of people coming and going. Soon it will be time to start and it promises to be an enjoyable evening. After the principal welcomes everyone, the head boy of the Sixth Form gives a little speech, reminding the growing audience of the vision for Jamaica – the whole room repeats it loudly – and the purpose of the concert. There is another quick greeting from a gentleman from the Peace and Love in Schools programme and then the M.C. takes over. He is a tall, lanky boy from Grade Ten, a born comedian, who soon has the audience roaring with laughter as he introduces each act. A lot of talent is on show from singing and deejay, to dances, poetry and more. The boys hoot loudly, the girls scream with laughter, and many take to the floor to enjoy the musical rhythms that punctuate the performances.

When Manny ascends the stage decked out like a parson in a long dark jacket, white shirt, a huge black and silver polka dot tie and bright yellow pants, there is a sudden but short-lived hush. Then the sight of the boy they call Countryman in the oversized jacket, the thick-rimmed glasses, and clutching a huge Bible under one arm, leads to peals of laughter and clapping. He is a comical sight to behold for his pants are also far too short to be called long pants and his shoes are twice the size of his feet. He has a serious scowl on his face despite the laughter around him. Having already scored with his costume Manny launches confidently into his well-rehearsed delivery of a sermon on overcoming challenges. He warms to his topic quickly, taking the audience through dramatic stories of Daniel, Moses and other icons from the Bible and what they did in the face of difficulties. He prances energetically across the stage, flailing his arms, slapping and waving the Holy Book to reinforce his points. Every couple of lines he punctuates his sermon with a drawn-out "Yesss Suh!" which his audience quickly catches on to and repeats in chorus. His tone is loud and gruff and his grammar lacking, which endears him to his 'congregation' even more. Amid the laughter, Manny brings home the point that many people can overcome their challenges through strength of will, determination and purpose. He bows to rousing applause at the end and exits the stage with a smile, to a slap on the back from his Drama teacher waiting in the wings.

The rest of the concert goes well and at the very end, the gentleman from Peace and Love in Schools comes back on stage to make some final comments. He speaks in a soft, gentle tone that hushes his audience to listen.

"When we stand at the school crossing and the cars and buses stop for us to cross the road safely...

"When we obey the rules about always being in the proper school uniform...

"When we stand in line and wait on the bus, or at the post office or clinic...

"Or when we solve our problems by sitting down and talking instead of fighting...

"...we are obeying the rule of law and order. We can think of many other examples. Some rules are backed by laws that have been made in our Parliament over many years, while others arise from our moral values, culture and way of life. We need discipline in order to obey rules in the society, including in school.

"When we live together in a community, we need to abide by the rule of law and order in everything we do. That is how our society will work best. If I were a driver, and I ignored all the red lights, then I would cause accidents and serious harm to people and myself. We can only imagine what would happen if every citizen of Jamaica and every student in our schools did exactly what they wanted to do, without any reward or punishment. Nothing would work, not even a school. There would be chaos. In the same

way, we should look at our schools as communities, and make sure there is peace and order.

"Let us all respect each other, no matter how different we may be. In our homes, schools and communities, we should live in harmony by obeying the rules that allow our society to work. School is as good a place as any to start. You have all done well here today, and I am proud to have been involved."

With that, the principal thanks everyone, and the concert comes to a noisy end. Students scatter about, chatting with each other, the boys vying for the attention of the girls from the other schools. Refreshment is served and the excitement of the evening lingers on even as the crowd begins to leave the hall. Manny joins his friends outside and they again congratulate him on his performance. Manny smiles broadly. He has also enjoyed himself. He knows his grand-aunt will be pleased when he relates the story to her. His father too and all the folks back home in the countryside will certainly get the full tale. He knows they will be proud of him and his involvement in school. Most of all, he knows they will see from his school report that he is making good strides in his work and getting good grades. Manny smiles again as he thinks to himself – take three giant steps. He looks up at the promise of a pink and gold sunset on the evening horizon.

"Yes," he vows, "I can do that."

VISION 2030 JAMAICA:
Jamaica, the place of choice to live, work, raise families and do business.

Poem: The Sun's Day

The sun rises silently behind the misty Blue Mountains in the east…

and slips into the western seas with a soft ripple, as
    evening wanes.

On its journey across our beautiful island

It nods to the beat of mento drums hailing the dawn,

and cheerful feet dancing off to school.

Colourful bodies sway to the rhythm of a busy new day,

As coconut palms give way to rolling green banana fields,

and acres of sweet, sweet sugarcane…

Piers and ports and long, snaking highways…

Hustle and bustle of bright towns and cities

Lend their roaring warmth and friendship to the doting sun as it rises high,

Striding confidently across plains and hills.

Sweet reggae rhythms embrace the coasts

Fishers and farmers here, tour guides and craftsmen there

They wink as the sun plays hide and seek between fluffy afternoon clouds…

Hilly, cool countryside and bread-basket farms

Bursting with colour, and birds winging home

Weary faces and places relax in the shadow of evening.

The journey over, the sun sighs with honest pleasure…

As it slides beneath shell-blue water…

Goodnight Jamaica,

Land I love…

see you in the morning.

Collette Robinson
January 2011

Activity

a. Can you trace the parishes as you follow the sun across the island?
b. Can you trace the time of day?
c. Which words help you to see pictures in the poem?
d. Which words help you to hear sounds?

Here are the answers for the activity on page 13.

pride	knowledge	dignity
vision	potential	family
economy	climate	plan
values	choice	environment

How many of them did you get correct?